C000053042

IMAGES OF ENGLAND

AROUND
GUISBOROUGH

IMAGES OF ENGLAND

AROUND
GUISBOROUGH

PAM WILSON

TEMPUS

Frontispiece: The author's grandparents, Fred and Charlotte (Lottie) Durrans pose for a family photograph with their daughters, Mary and Violet. A painter and decorator by trade, Fred was the treasurer for the Congregational chapel in Westgate for many years and also helped his wife to run the shop on Park View Terrace at the end of Allison Street.

First published 2003

Tempus Publishing Limited
The Mill, Brimscombe Port,
Stroud, Gloucestershire, GL5 2QG

© Pam Wilson, 2003

The right of Pam Wilson to be identified as the Author of this work has been asserted in accordance with the Copyrights, Designs and Patents Act 1988.

All rights reserved. No part of this book may be reprinted or reproduced or utilised in any form or by any electronic, mechanical or other means, now known or hereafter invented, including photocopying and recording, or in any information storage or retrieval system, without the permission in writing from the Publishers.

British Library Cataloguing in Publication Data.
A catalogue record for this book is available from the British Library.

ISBN 0 7524 3075 0

Typesetting and origination by Tempus Publishing Limited
Printed in Great Britain by Midway Colour Print, Wiltshire

Contents

The Quartercentury service at the Priory, June 1961. On the platform on the left is the Rector Morrison, in the centre the Bishop of Whitby and on the right the headmaster of the Grammar School Mr J.A. Bruce. Back row, from left to right, staff of the school are; Mr N.R. Stephenson, W.N. Thompson, Mr T.W. Burdon, -?- , -?- , Mr W.P. Cooper.

Introduction

Once a small, rural agricultural market town of blacksmiths, coopers, leather and linen workers, Guisborough began to expand in the latter half of the nineteenth century with the advent of iron mining, which provided employment for many men and boys. People travelled great distances at that time looking for work, with the result that many Guisborough families today – part of my own included – are descended from miners who settled here from as far away as Lincolnshire, Norfolk and Cornwall.

In the early twentieth century came the closure of the ironstone mines, and although there was employment for some at The Foundry, the iron foundry owned by Blackett Hutton, there was a shortage of jobs until Imperial Chemical Industries opened at Wilton. Once again the town expanded, and many fields were taken for the building of houses to accommodate the influx of employees of ICI.

Many changes have taken place in Guisborough during the twentieth century; long established businesses have closed, buildings have been altered beyond recognition, some old streets demolished, and the foundry and the shirt factory are both consigned to history. The spirit of Guisborough still survives though, and a walk along Westgate on a market day has the same friendly feeling that it had fifty years ago, even on a cold wintry day when the wind whistles along with the malicious intention of whipping the canopy from every stall in its path.

The history of Guisborough has been well documented and this book makes no pretension to being a fully factual account, but is merely a nostalgic look back at people, events and the way that the town has changed.

There is something very special about Guisborough that never lets people forget their roots, calling it 'home' although they may have lived on the far side of the world for the majority of their adult lives. No matter where in the world you travel, it is surprising how many people you will meet who have relatives or friends here, or have even lived here themselves once.

Guisborough would not be the same without the remains of the Priory, but its history is well recorded and thus this book simply shows some of the more contemporary ways in which the Priory grounds have been, and still are, used.

Acknowledgements

Thanks go to all the people who have helped in some way with the compilation of this book; whether they loaned photographs, shared memories or put me in touch with others who could help, they showed a true Gisborian spirit, and I hope they enjoy the result. This book is for them, and in memory of those who went before us.

Thanks first to Stuart Burns who sent me to Pat's Barber Shop in Chaloner Street to see their collection of old photographs, which, naturally enough, I had never had occasion to see before. So, thanks go to Pat Pearson and John Devonport. The contacts I made from there were invaluable, such as Mr Edmund Phillips who provided me with all the pictures for Chapter Two. I have been unable to trace the owners of the originals of a few photographs, and hope that I cause no offence in using them. Thanks also go to Colin Smiley of Prior Pursglove College for his help with the Grammar School archives.

Vera Bailey, Mr Ron Boyes, Mr John Brelstaff, Mrs Mary Brown, Mr Syd Carey, Mr H. Copping, Fred and Elaine Dadd, Moira Carter, Mark Seaton, Margaret Darnton, Barry and Dot Dixon, Ron Durrans, Joan Easton, the Garbutt family, Rachel Hart, Jean Jones, Peter Lillie, Mr Neil and Miss Marion Macdonald, George and Barbara McGee, Doreen and Neil Newson, Harold Oliver, Jean Sanderson, Mrs Betty Sayer, Dick Scott, Mr R.R. Seaton, Mrs Lilian Smith, Paul Smith, Bertha Spinks, Trudi Thorpe, John Topham, Dave Trigg, Mr Bernard Wilkinson, Lily and Malcolm Wilks, Dave Willerton, Brian Wynn and Mrs Young all loaned photographs or gave information for which I am grateful.

Thanks also to the gentlemen of the 'Men Only' bar of the Quoit Club for information and names to accompany some of the photographs.

Last but not least, thanks go to my family; my son Paul Smith who is my most helpful critic, his wife Maureen, my granddaughter Jenny and my other sons Duncan and Alec Smith. They have all been very patient and suffered a lack of attention for the last few months while the preparation of this book has taken priority.

one

Around
Guisborough

Children of the orphanage in Park Lane during the 1930s. Violet Durrans is the young carer at the back on the right, and in front of her, with a stranglehold on his friend is Rudolph Hector Outhwaite. No other names are available, although one of the boys is probably Billy Tinkler who kept in touch with Violet all her life.

The market cross is decorated here for a celebration of some kind. Always a popular place for festivities, the cross and the entrances leading to Church Street and Bow Street were frequently decorated with garlands.

Above: Although fox hunting is now a highly controversial subject, this was not the case in 1922 when this photograph of 'the meet' was taken by the market cross.

Right: Richard Durrans on the front doorstep of No. 39 Allison Street in 1911. The first child of Fred and Lottie, he was born in 1908 and died at the age of four from scarlet fever, in the isolation hospital at the top of Belmangate.

The cobbled back street behind Allison Street and Park View Terrace provided a playground for young Ron Durrans in 1926. Note the 'midden' doors where the 'night soil' was removed from the earth closets.

These children (including on the left a young Carey), are standing in the old 'Fair Field' on Redcar Road, and in the background is the police station. There are still many people in Guisborough who have fond memories of the fair with its stalls and roundabouts, goldfish in bowls, toffee apples, candy floss and mud. Always mud! In 1909 the infant school log book records that the headmaster had 'received notice to close tomorrow, Tuesday 26 April, for the Fair' – no doubt in acceptance of the fact that there would be no attendees at school anyway.

Looking down Redcar Road from the police station area, it seems as though everyone was waiting for something. Perhaps a procession was on the way, or a funeral was wending its way to the cemetery.

The fire station in Fountain Street at around the turn of the century – it is now a restaurant.

Above: This crowd in Guisborough market place are gathered to celebrate the Coronation of King George V.

Left: Grandma Boyes, resplendent in a fur coat, stands in Bird's Yard with her bags packed. However, her remaining family is unsure where she was going, and have written the query on the photograph. It is thought that she may have been moving house.

Right: John Robert Boyes with his children, Averil, Victor, Steve and Bertha (with her dolly) outside their home in Bird's Yard in the 1930s.

Below: Houses in Bird's Yard, *c.* 1930. (Photograph by the late Mr W.D. Brelstaff)

Sydney, Percy and Eva Carey stand outside their home in Church Street in July 1935. Perhaps they were ready for the celebrations of King George the V's Silver Jubilee as the boys are in their smart Boy Scout uniforms.

Sixty-six years later, Syd's granddaughter Jenny Smith stands outside the same building, which has managed to survive until 2003 without change – on the outside at least.

Above: Taken around 1920, this photograph shows the Three Fiddles and the Provident Industrial Society (the Co-op) butchering department (left). Standing at the left of the pub's front door is Harry Davis, the proprietor, and the other figure is believed to be Tom Scott who owned the seed merchant shop a little higher up Westgate. Through the archway was a yard containing two cottages which adjoined and were owned by the public house. The large sign on the pub reads 'Entirely Free House, Three Fiddles Inn, Trés Bon Beer. Harry Davis, proprietor', and the one above the door reads; 'Harry Davis, licensed to retail British and Foreign Spirits, Wines, etc. Ale, Porter and Tobacco'.

To the left of the door is a declaration that 'These premises are permitted to be open between 10 a.m. and 10 p.m. every Tuesday'.

Right: Bernard Wilkinson, Harry Davis' grandson, riding his first car in the yard behind the Three Fiddles.

Three little boys enjoying life on an old builders handcart in the yard of the Three Fiddles, around 1930.

Violet Durrans takes a break from serving in her parents' shop on Park View Terrace, 1930.

Right: The fence opposite the shop was obviously a popular place for posing. Trudi, Mary and Ron Durrans with a friend stand with their backs to the field that is now occupied by the infant school.

Below: The eerie silence brought by snow in the deserted market place can almost be felt in this picture, which was taken around 1930.

Above: Tuesday at Guisborough was cattle auction day, when farm animals were taken to the mart in Union Street to be checked, weighed, bought and sold. All the public houses in Guisborough had extended opening hours on these days and it was very busy, with farmers coming to town from the outlying villages. At the turn of the twentieth century, a butcher regularly travelled by horse and cart from Middlesbrough to buy cattle for slaughter. Once his transactions were complete his employee herded the beasts along the winding road to Middlesbrough, while he himself retired to the King's Head for the remainder of the day, at the end of which he then collapsed onto his cart where he slept, drunk as a lord, and relied upon his horse to take him home.

Inside the cattle mart at the top of the picture are Francis Rose and David Holmes, with Ramsay Hall on the right, Fred Suckling on the left and Dennis Covell and Freddie Dobson standing at the desk. The photograph was taken by a pupil from Laurence Jackson School, Adrian Porritt, under the supervision of Mr John Brelstaff.

Opposite, above: Behind this row of houses on Fountain Street and the public toilets at the bottom of Bow Street stood the railway station. All of these buildings were demolished many years ago, leaving room for a Health Centre which was later built on this site.

Opposite, below: How strange the market place looks without the cross – empty and characterless! At this time in the 1970s, it had been the victim of an accident and was removed for repair.

On very hot summer days when the temperature inside the shirt factory was becoming oppressive, a decision would be taken by management to vacate the building for a short break. The buzzer would be sounded, followed by a welcome announcement to go outside into the fresh air and within minutes there would be bodies sprawled leisurely about the garden, enjoying the fresh air and a gossip. This photograph of the staff is more formal, however, and was taken on a day trip to Scarborough in the late 1940s. Those pictured include: Johnnie and Nora Cowley with baby Michael; Jim (Jammer) Covell; Freda

Stephenson; Brenda Bearpark; the Gargett brothers; Sylvia Brown; Edna Dunning; Betsy Williams; ? Swales; Tommy, Ruby and 'Tut' Thompson; Joyce Irwin; Cynthia and Joyce Dewing; Dolly Mann; Lily Wilson; Margaret Grange; Joyce Fowler; Iris and Sheila Lumsden; Helen and Cynthia Oakley; Rosa Ditchburn; Mildred Jeffels; Isa Knaggs; Ellen Graham; Eva Dewing; Mary Towers; Betty Rodham; Edgar Covell; Iris Ditchburn; Amy Towers and Ruth Jeffels.

Guisborough
SHIRT COMPANY LIMITED

DINNER, WHIST DRIVE AND DANCE
COATHAM HOTEL, REDCAR, THURSDAY, DECEMBER 22nd, 1949

Keep this programme — you may win a free holiday

This was not the winning programme, (the prize in a raffle being a holiday) but one that was kept by Lily Wilks as a souvenir of the shirt factory dinner and dance at the Coatham Hotel in Redcar, Christmas 1949.

Above: The exact occasion or location is unclear, but these people were certainly members of the Territorial Army out on a day trip in about 1956. Only a few have been identified, including 'Mop' Jackson, Jack Swales, Harry Edwards, Jimmy Swales and Averil Boyes.

Opposite, below: During its lifetime, the clothing factory changed owners and names several times, but to the people of Guisborough it was always referred to as 'the shirt factory'. It provided employment for many people over the years and this photograph shows a happy workforce just before Christmas, sometime in the mid–1950s. A few of the girls have been identified: Betty Antil, Emily Thompson, Phyllis Barr, Mona Lynn and M. Towers.

Above: At No. 2 Redcar Road in 1981, the veterinary surgeons Ian Macdonald BVMS MRCVS, Neil Macdonald MRCVS, Michael Dobson and Angus Tosh gathered for the retirement of Phyllis Carey (Evans) as receptionist and practice secretary. Mr Neil Macdonald came from Altrincham and began the veterinary practice in Redcar Road in 1933, where he was joined later by his son Ian.

Opposite, above: Dutch elm disease claimed what was once a fine tree in the grounds of the Priory.

Opposite, below: The diseased elm tree reduced to a pile of logs.

Mr E. Phillips captured these four images of the demolition of a row of railway houses in Fountain Street in the mid-1960s. The name on the bulldozer is Kirkby Bros.

Down it comes!

On the left of this image the building that was once the fire station can just be seen, and the house on Bow Street where Derek Richardson, the photographer, lived and had his business.

The railway houses in Fountain Street reduced to rubble, *c.* 1967.

There can hardly have been a little boy growing up in Guisborough in the 1960s who did not love to take a walk up Butt Lane and scramble onto 'The Tank', a relic from the days when the army used this area of the hills for exercises and target practise. It lay at the foot of the hills rusting slowly away for many years until the 1970s when it was removed for scrap. It was very sadly missed. There was also a row of 'butts' (targets) here, which gave the name to Butt Lane. Unable to trace the original owners of this photograph, the author thanks in their absence the Garbutt family, and hopes that they do not mind being portrayed in the book!

The Cleveland Hills which provide many good walks, as viewed from Stump Cross.

Looking from Kemplah towards Highcliff and the hills.

Before they were taken over for development, the Kemplah fields were popular for walking, playing and picnics in the summer and, as is illustrated here, were good for sledging in the winter.

Fred and Lottie Durrans with daughter Trudi, son Ronnie and friends, enjoying a lazy summer afternoon in Kemplah fields in 1928.

During the summer months many horses were grazed in Kemplah fields, as can be seen here in 1965, behind Mandy Carey and Gavin Brelstaff.

Duncan and Alec Smith in Kemplah fields, *c.* 1974.

Taken from the bridge that once carried the railway line to Whitby, this photograph shows new housing under construction on Rievaulx Way, Whitby Avenue and Handale Close, during the summer of 1969.

Paul Smith and Nigel Edwards taking advantage of a lull in the traffic on Rievaulx Way a little later!

Elaine Fawcett and her sister Mary have just completed their shopping here at Ernie Alcock's fruit shop, which stood next door to the Three Fiddles. A lady is peering out of the window behind them – perhaps Mrs Alcock – to see what is going on.

Ernie Alcock stands outside his shop with his assistants Mary Fawcett and Nellie Whitworth.

Johnson's Yard shortly before demolition in 2003.

Above: Drew's bus depot in Wilson Street before demolition in 2002.

Right: This listed building, No. 36 Redcar Road, was formerly known as the Park Hotel. In the 1930s, the front room of this house was used as Dr Fulton's surgery.

The exterior appearance of the King's Head has changed very little since this photograph was taken and is still splendid with the original tiles on the front wall. Decorated with flags to celebrate a royal occasion, it could possibly be King George V's Coronation in 1910.

In the year 2000, shortly before being sold, No.80 Westgate stood in its original state amid the shops and businesses.

Less than three years later, the building had a short career as an Indian takeaway before being gutted by a fire.

Number 144 Westgate still remains unspoilt by modernisation.

The pleasant little park at the side of Westgate was latterly known by many as 'Titty-bottle Park', no doubt because it was mainly frequented by young mums with their offspring who happily passed time on the swings and see-saws. This photograph was taken by Paul Smith from an upstairs window of no. 144 Westgate.

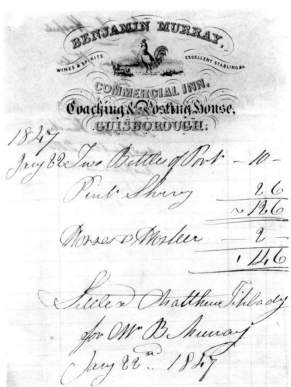

This receipt from the Cock Inn reads: 'Benjamin Murray, Commercial Inn, coaching and Posting House. 1847. Two bottles of port 10s. One pint of sherry 2s 6d, horses and Ostler 2s'.

Above: Tockett's Mill in around 1930, while in use by the Seaton family. The mill ceased production in 1960. In 1972 the mill and and house became vacant and restoration began in 1975 and was completed in 1982.

Opposite, above: Lizzie Seaton stands in the doorway of Tockett's Mill, *c.* 1930. Her father William Henry Seaton was the miller, and two of his sons, Arthur and Percy, delivered grain and flour by horse and cart to the neighbouring villages and Guisborough.

Opposite, below: Arthur Seaton delivering goods from the mill.

Barnaby Pit on the moors. Although rather isolated, Barnaby had its own school and church.

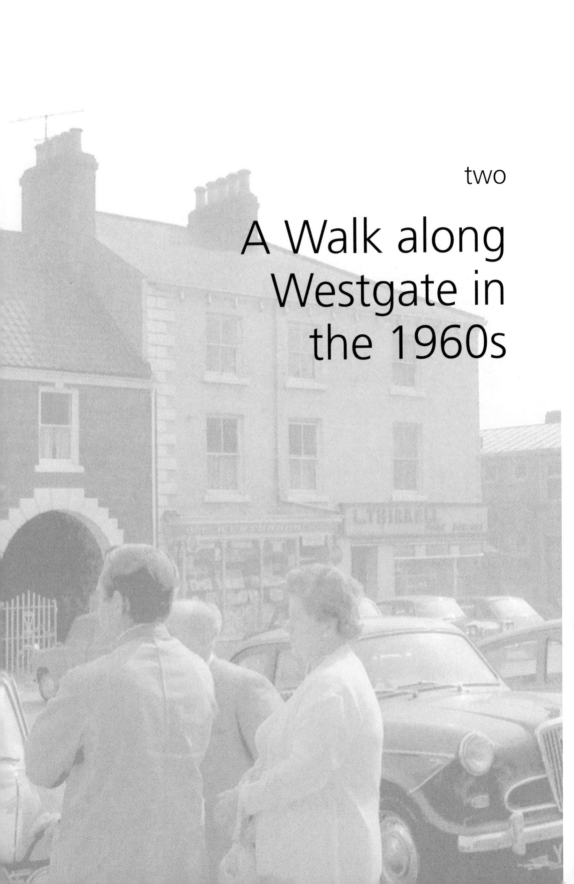

two

A Walk along Westgate in the 1960s

Above: The following series of photographs provides us with a unique opportunity to put back the clock almost forty years. They were taken by Mr Edmund Phillips who, luckily for us, had popped a film into his new camera and decided to test its performance by snapping pictures of the shops as he walked along Westgate. Shall we take a walk with him along memory lane? We begin our walk at Metcalfe's (above) with a look at the newspapers in the window, and then on to Greenwood's the chemist with its windows full of bottles and a large advertisement for Kodak film above the door.

Left: Round the corner stands the National Provincial Bank, and the wrought-iron gate through which a photograph was taken as war began in 1939. (The photograph on page 67 was taken from inside the gate at the bank).

Time for a leisurely chat outside Tom Pallister's butcher shop before crossing over the top of Bow Street to Norman Robinson's newsagent shop for tobacco or a paper, and then across to the Seven Stars.

Beyond the market cross is the Town Hall (right), and behind that can just seen the cottages of Bakehouse Square.

Travelling along the 'bottom side', we get a full view of the Town Hall with the arched windows on the ground floor enclosing what was once an open market.

Meadows' sweet shop and Seatory's butchers join the Mermaid Inn.

Pullars the dry cleaners next, followed by Hintons grocery store. The vehicle in the foreground is an Austin A40 van.

Waiting for a bus outside the Chocolate Box must have been rather tempting with all those jars of sweets: Nebo Creams, Soor Plooms, Sherbet Lemons, Cherry Lips, and Kali with a stick of Spanish…

47

A. Gray & Son was the place to go when you needed a pram or a bicycle.

The archway (opposite) still had its gate across in the 1960s, on to Westbrook's newsagents, then next door was Thirkell's butcher shop and in the background the 'new' post office.

A few yards further along. A contrast of fashions with the elderly ladies in the background, and the young woman wearing modern trousers and with her hair in the 'latest' bee-hive hairstyle.

The lady standing on the left is a conductress, or 'Clippie', from a bus, taking a breath of air. (These ladies had ticket machines and cash bags strapped round them and walked the length of the bus collecting fares, for those who do not remember). The old houses in Chaloner Street shown here stand almost untouched by commerce, though Mr Reily's opticians can just be seen.

Above, left: The post office is busy and Chaloner Street is almost blocked by a lorry. The last house to be seen clearly here is where Mr and Mrs Young lived with the telephone exchange in their front room.

Above, right: Past the post office and the telephone boxes we reach a house (on the right) that is soon to be demolished.

Once Pybus' Funeral Directors, the building is soon to make way for Boots the Chemist. The sign reads: 'New prestige Shopping Parade to be erected on this site (52ft frontage) Enquiries to the agents Albert Walker and son'. In the 1960s the Mini was a very popular car, easy to park in small spaces, as shown outside the post office.

Above: Here we cross over to the top side and close on our heels is Elaine Fawcett (wearing trousers), carefully watching for traffic as she crosses the road from Ivy Walker's.

Right: The old cottages where Nellie Hughes once lived have been demolished, making room for, as the sign reads, 'New Showrooms and Workshops. Mackinlay Hyde Motors.'

We're coming up to Dr Pratt's surgery door now (the ground floor of the old cottages); there was no appointment system in those days, you simply arrived at the surgery, and waited for your turn.

Still referred to as 'Dr Pratt's' the house stands on the corner of Westgate Road, and on the opposite corner is Sunnyfield House. Both look just the same in 2003.

Right: Once the home of Dr Stainthorpe, Sunnyfield House has had several uses over the years, including a Housing Office and Planning Department of Langbaurgh Council.

Below: The Three Fiddles comes into view now (right), with gates closed over what was once the entrance to two cottages.

Slightly obscured by the tree is Ernie Alcock's fruit shop, adjoining Myers. The bus travelling along Westgate was probably the 'Green Line', heading for Great Ayton and Stokesley.

The ornamental iron gates between Myers' shoe shop and Jeffels' hardware once led to the Wesleyan chapel, which stood where the car park is today.

Let's call in at Olga Page's for some embroidery thread or knitting wool, or perhaps a new blouse...
then a Wall's ice cream next door, or shall we save the money instead and pop in to see Mr Flounders
at the York County Savings Bank?

There's quite a queue of people at the bus stop outside the Fine Fare supermarket, some with shopping
bags full of bargains: according to the posters on the window, sugar is only 1s and $2\frac{1}{2}$d at Fine Fare this
week, dairy butter 2s 11d, Nescafe 4s and P.G. Tips tea 1s 4d.

Between Leeming's chemist and Shipman's bakery is the snicket, which led to the old Priory Hall where many a party and dance was held, and ballet lessons too, before it was destroyed in a fire. Farther along Westgate are the Orange Café and the Black Swan.

On the corner of Northgate stands Meredith's, the building that once housed Galanti's ice cream parlour. Next is Jaydor Fashions and Moore's groceries. At this point the author halts and gets a shock. Could that be me crossing the road with son number one, Paul, in his pushchair? If so, that defines the year that these photographs were taken: it must be 1966!

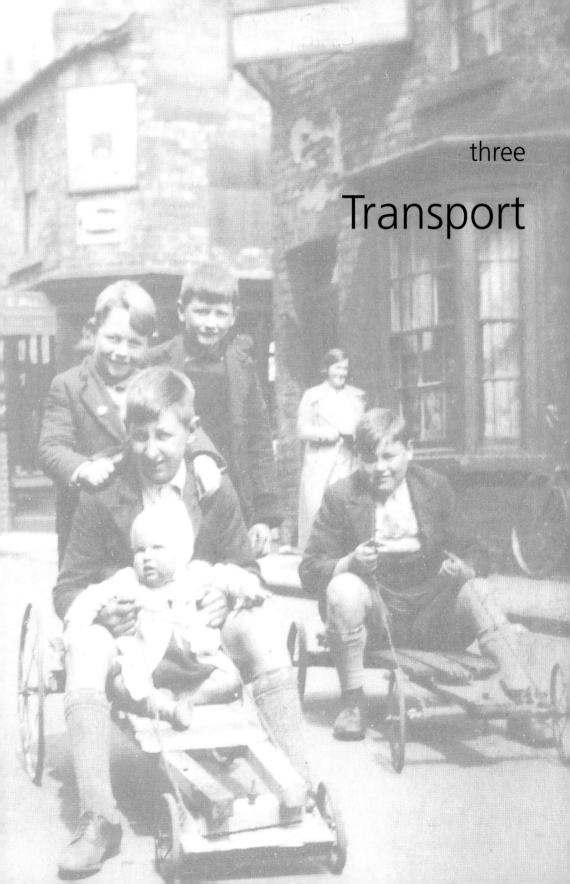

three

Transport

Above: Richardson and Scurlock garage at the bottom of Belmangate was demolished, possibly in the early 1960s, to make way for a new petrol station which was itself eventually removed to widen the road. At the time that the road was altered, the first house on Belmangate, shown here behind the garage, was also demolished and a deep well was found on the land. This photo of the snow-bound garage was taken during one of the severe winters of the 1960s.

Opposite, below: The Dobson family from Charltons ran a bus company, and this was their charabanc, seen here taking employees of the Co-op store on a trip to Scarborough.

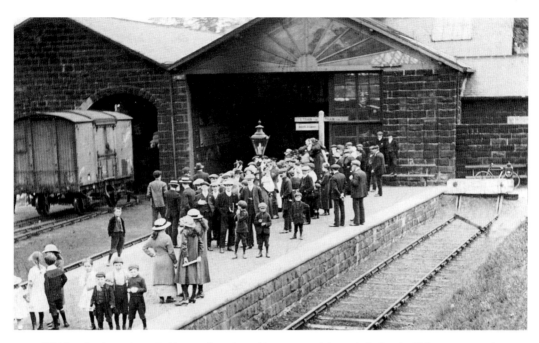

Waiting for the train at Guisborough station, this group anticipate their Quoit Club summer outing, in around 1912.

A primitive form of transport, but great fun, was the 'bogey'. Discarded prams or push chairs – in fact anything with wheels, were soon recycled by boys with an inventive streak and, with the addition of a few pieces of wood, turned into racing cars! These children must have chosen the most dangerous street in Guisborough to play with bogies – Cleveland Street running so steeply as it does, straight down onto Westgate. From left to right the children are: Ray Bentley and Les Tyreman; in front are Stan Dobson and Billy Hill, but the lady and the baby are unknown. In the background is the Miners Arms public house.

The Dobson bus, named the 'Charltonian' because of the family connection with Charltons, is shown parked in front of Medd's and Smith's at Saltburn. According to the sign on the front of the bus it is heading next for Castleton and Danby.

George and Mary Cleaver astride their motorbike with 'Granddad' Cleaver riding in style in the sidecar, *c.* 1930.

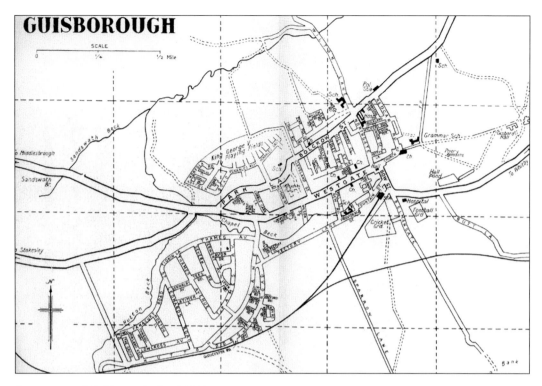

A street map of Guisborough, dated 1960.

Ladies from the Congregational chapel on a coach trip in the late 1930s. Mrs Durrans is on the right with her daughter Mary, who was organist for the chapel for many years, and granddaughters Brenda and Kathleen are in the centre.

The winters of the 1960s were severe, with the Whitby Moor road closed by drifts of snow several times. For many days there were no milk deliveries through to Guisborough so the younger, fitter residents of the Whitby Lane estate took it in turn to struggle over snowdrifts 10ft deep on Butt Lane to fetch milk from the farm.

The North Yorkshire Council snow plough arriving on Whitby Lane to clear the road.

Above: At the end of Bolckow Street stands the Catholic church St Paulinus, and the vacant plot where the new petrol station is about to be built.

Left: Billy Young, the owner of the new garage and petrol station at the end of Hollymead Drive, fills up a motorcycle with fuel.

four

Wartime

Boy soldiers being inspected at Guisborough Grammar School.

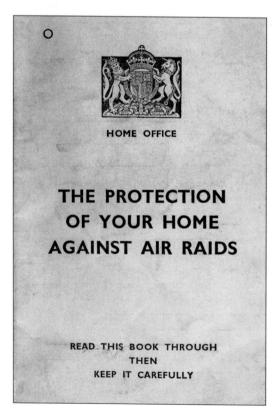

HOME OFFICE

THE PROTECTION OF YOUR HOME AGAINST AIR RAIDS

READ THIS BOOK THROUGH
THEN
KEEP IT CAREFULLY

This booklet was published in 1938 by the Home Office, priced one penny, and gives full instructions on how to protect your home against air raids. It was kept as a reminder by Malcolm Wilks, although he hoped not to need it again after 1945. Once a refuge room was prepared with essentials including candles and matches, scissors and brown paper, food etc., families were advised to keep a wireless or receiver to listen to the news and pass the time away.

Taken at 11.00 a.m. on Sunday 3 September 1939 as the Second World War started, this picture was taken as a record in case the town was destined to suffer damage. The library can be seen on the right, also Scott's, the Co-op (Provident Industrial Society) and Moore's Stores.

Looking out from the Priory grounds onto Church Street at 11.00 a.m., 3 September 1939.

A large group of Guisborough men at the railway station prepare to go to war in 1914.

'The Villains of Handale Camp'.
Left to right: Sgt R. Scaife, ?
Flanary, ? Watson and ? Brett
(Sooty).

The only soldiers identified here are Fred Durrans, front
left, and Sgt Ripley centre front, again at Gosforth Park.

69

Guisborough members of the Green Howards at Gosforth Park. From left to right, back row: -?- , Fred Bulmer (who lived in an old cottage on Belmangate), -?-, -?- , -?- . Front row: -?- , -?- , Fred Durrans, -?- .

On the doorstep of No. 10, Walker's Row, Harriet Wilson poses with her son Jack who was home on leave from the army, around 1942.

Young ladies of the Wrens on 12 May 1944 at their training ground, HMS Fledgling at Millmeece in Staffordshire. Bertha Boyes of Guisborough is first left (seated).

A New Year greetings postcard sent from 'somewhere on active service', 14 December 1918, by Tom Boyes to his brother Jack in Cleveland Street.

Guisborough Territorial Army. Back row, from left to right: D. Hoggarth, F. Richardson, C. Dale. Middle row: S. Jackson, I. Bell, F. Topham, R. Davison, B. Dale, -?- . Front row: Gordon Carey, N. Jackson, ? Thorpe, R. Boyes, ? Bickmore, R. Hill, ? Patterson, B. Mitchell.

An Armistice Day parade outside Sunnyfield House, possibly in 1980. From the left: -?- , -?- , Jackie Swales, ? Boyes, George McMurdough, Jack Carter, -?- , -?- , -?- , -?- , Jack Hassan, -?- , -?- , Dickie Rodham, John Thirsk, Mr Hart.

The Lord Mayor's Dance at Sunnyfield House. The entertainment for the evening was provided by a Barber Shop Choir from Middlesbrough. Fifth from left, in the centre row is Sydney Carey, and sixth from left is the Lord Mayor of the time, Bob Hoggarth.

A wartime listening post on the moors above Hutton village.

five

Churches, Chapels and Weddings

Above: Mr Copping leads the Salvation Army band as they march along Fountain Street, where they had premises before the new citadel was built.

Opposite, above: Women of the Wesleyan church in their Sunday best gather at Barnaby Moor on 12 June 1912. Second from the right on the back row is Margaret Carey Lister, but the rest remain unnamed.

Opposite, below: The Salvation Army band of Guisborough, *c.* 1920.

William Wilson, the author's grandfather, in his uniform of the Salvation Army band. William was the youngest member of the band at the time, being only eighteen years of age.

Kathy Readman (left) and Violet Durrans (right), with little Trudi Durrans. This and the following three images were all taken on a Sunday school trip from Guisborough Congregational chapel to Saltburn.

Taken in the 1920s, this photograph shows Mr Stanley, the Congregational Minister from Guisborough and some of the Sunday school children enjoying their annual trip. Back row from left to right: Kathy Readman, -?- , Gibson Sayer (who played cricket and football for Guisborough), and Robert ? Mason. Front row: Harold Sunley, Trudi Durrans, and somewhere beneath the large hat is Ronald Durrans!

Above: The wedding of Steve Wilson and Violet Durrans on 29 May 1939 at the Ebenezer Congregational chapel on Westgate.

Opposite, above: At this time the pier at Saltburn was still intact with sheltered seats at the far end where it was pleasant to sit and watch the sea, while being protected on three sides from the wind.

Opposite, below: A fine group of Guisborough lads with the Sunday school trip enjoying a paddle in the sea at Saltburn, *c.* 1928. On the front row (right) is Ronnie Durrans.

A wedding at the Wesleyan chapel on 26 July 1947. This chapel stood on the land which is now a car park behind a health food shop, before being demolished in the mid-1960s. Bride and groom are Ken Monkhouse and Nellie Poskett and bridesmaids were? Armin, Betty Matthews, ? Monkhouse and Bertha Boyes. On the wall to the left is a plaque that reads, 'This stone was laid by Mrs Lynas November 17th' – the year is very indistinct but looks like 1824.

The approach to St Nicholas' church was, until quite recently, adorned by well-kept flowerbeds.

Bertha Boyes in her beautiful wedding dress beside St Nicholas' church. During the war all clothing was on coupons and for most people a wedding dress was something to be borrowed or to do without. Luckily Bertha had a friend with contacts at Elstree Studios and the result was that she was loaned this elegant pink satin dress for her important day. As she says, 'It didn't matter that it was pink as it looked white on the photographs, anyway'.

Mary Ann and John Robert Boyes celebrate their Golden Wedding Day in Stokeld's garden. Stokeld's had a printing business in Fountain Street and Mary Ann had been in service to a member of their family, while her husband John Robert kept their garden tended in his spare time.

Opposite, above: Brenda Boyes arrives for her marriage at St Nicholas' church, with a busy Church Street in the background.

Opposite, below: The wedding of Frank Jones and Jean Seaton in 1955 at St Paulinus' Catholic church. Fom left to right are: Mrs Lena Bennett, Mrs Lilian Seaton, Babs Brown, Peter Hewling, Frank Jones, Jean Seaton, Eric Bennett, Gwen Wilkinson and Robert Roland (Roley) Seaton.

Right: In August 1963 a bride makes her way to the Ebenezer Congregational chapel, while in the background is Darnton's butchers shop.

Left: August 1963 a couple of newly-weds leave Belmont Terrace for their honeymoon in Scotland. Well-wishers from left to right are: John Williamson, June Williamson, Harriet Wilson, Mary Cleaver, Margaret Cleaver, the winner of the bride's bouquet Anne Haley, Delia Jackson, Steve Wilson, Ken Jackson, Carole Cleaver, Lily Wilks, Pat Wilson and Jack Wilson.

The Methodist church on the south side, or the bottom side, of Westgate.

Elizabeth Dadd and Stephen Limon on their wedding day in 1980. The Priory grounds have for many years been a popular setting for wedding photographs.

six

Recreation
and Sport

The Clown Band in 1935 at the celebrations of King George V's Jubilee. This band also played for charity functions around the town and raised a considerable amount of money for good causes.

The Boyes brothers Tom and Jack, with their friend 'Mouser', proudly display their cycling prizes.

Right: This advertisement for entertainment at the Cock Inn reads: 'Juvenile Harpists Adolphus, Earnest and Fanny Lockwood give two concerts on 18 July 1850, front seats 2s, back seats 1s'.

Opposite, below: The opening of Guisborough Boys' Club 1937/8. Back row, from left to right: J. Walker, Revd.Wilken, -?- , Dr T.A. Pratt, Lord Gisborough, Cmdr. Bower, Sir William Worsley, Lady Gisborough, Lady Worsley, Mrs Donkin, -?- , Bob Jardine. Third row: Mr and Mrs Brown, Mrs Postgate, Mrs Jardine. Second row: A. Clements, H. Rurke, R. Breeze, H. Sherwood, N. Robinson, A. Barnard, Jack Wilson, G. Postgate, D. Clements, T. Holland, ? Gaines. Front row: B. Peggs, G. Corner, S. Waterson, W. Drew, S. Postgate, ? Postgate. The Boys' Club later became, and still remains, the Sea Cadets.

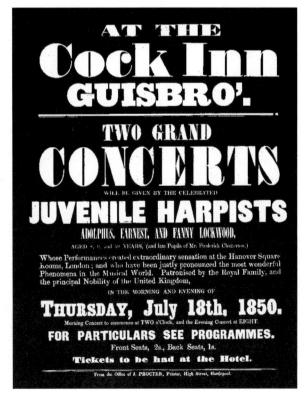

Concerts were given regularly in the Temperance Hall, with the performers coached by Mrs Lister and Mrs Smith. Mrs Smith's husband had the tailor shop near the Town Hall, on the bottom side, and Mrs Lister had a shop on Westgate. Mrs Mary Brown tells us that 'Mr and Mrs Lister lived on Westgate at the top of Parker's Yard, and it was here that the practises for the concerts took place; boys one night and girls another (but the boys hung around outside the window when it was girls' night and the girls did the same when it was the boys' turn!). We gave performances in the Temperance Hall and at all the villages round about, where we were provided with good suppers afterwards'. Back, left to right are Mrs Collinson, Mrs Lister, Mrs Smith, ? Bird. Front left to right; ? Smith, ? Devon, ? Smith, Ethel Byers and Mary Easby.

Above: Ernie Alcock with children on a carnival float in 1952.

Right: 'Stop me and buy one!' John Boyes in fancy dress as an ice cream seller adjusts the cornet on his son Victor's head, while Steve and Brenda sit in the ice cream cart, at Guisborough carnival in the mid-1930s.

Opposite, below: This performance of *Snow White and the Seven Dwarfs* was given in the Empire Theatre (the Picture House) around 1929. At the very back are Mrs Postgate and Mrs Catton, who coached the young girls. From left to right: Flora Barker, –?– , –?– , –?–, Dorothy Milburn, –? –, –?– , –?– , –?– , Mary Easby, –?– , –?– , –?– , –?– , –?– , –?– , Elsie Thompson, Ethel Byers, Violet Durrans, Mary Catton, –?– . The third dwarf from the right is Lilian Jackson, and the rest unfortunately remain unidentified.

Above: Trevor Buckworth braves the flames!

Opposite, above: Trevor Buckworth of the 'Ossalots' display team riding in the Motorcycle Gymkhana at the King George V playing field in the 1970s. Standing on the far right, sporting his fashionable hairstyle, is George McGee.

Opposite, below: Another member of the display team, Alan Smith, prepares for a daring leap, while the brave (or foolish) person beneath the ramp risks his life!

RULES.

1—That the Club be called "THE GUISBOROUGH CRICKET CLUB."

2—That the business of the Club, including the making and altering of Rules, shall be conducted by a Committee of 8 members (to be elected by ballot) and the Officers of the Club, all of whom shall be elected at the Annual General Meeting. In the event of any vacancy occurring in the Committee after such Annual Meeting the next in the order of voting to be elected.

3—That the Committee shall fix their own days of Meeting for the transaction of business, and at such Meeting 5 shall form a quorum.

4—That the Annual General Meeting shall be held not later than December in each year, of which Meeting 7 days' notice shall be given.

5—That the Annual Subscription be 7/6, which must be paid not later than the last day of May in each year.

6—That each year, on the receipt of the Annual Subscription, the Secretary shall forward to each Member his "Annual Ticket," which must be produced to the Gatekeeper at all matches, or in default the Member must pay the entrance fee as charged to the general public.

7—That a list of the Members of the Club shall be written out annually and hung up in the Pavilion

8—That an Extraordinary General Meeting may be called by notice in writing to the Secretary, signed by 12 Members of the Club, such Meeting to be called within 14 days after receipt of the notice.

9—That the Rules of the Club be printed along with the Matches arranged, and any infraction of such Rules shall be immediately dealt with by the Committee.

GUISBRO

Cricket Club

SEASON 1895.

J. T. STOKELD, PRINTER, GUISBROUGH.

A Guisborough Cricket Club membership card for 1895, for which the annual subscription at that time was 7s 6d.

First Eleven Fixtures.

DATE.	NAME OF CLUB.	WHERE PLAYED	RESULT For	Agt
May 4	Redcar*	away		
,, 11	Ironopolis*	home		
,, 18	Middlesbrough*	away		
,, 25	Stockton	home		
June 1	West Hartlepool*	away		
,, 4	Middlesbrough*	home		
,, 8	Constable Burton*	home		
,, 15	Ironopolis*	away		
,, 22	Great Ayton	home		
,, 29	Thirsk*	away		
July 6	Constable Burton*	away		
,, 13	West Hartlepool	home		
,, 20	Northallerton*	home		
,, 27	Thornaby*	home		
Aug. 3	Thirsk*	home		
,, 10	Great Ayton	home		
,, 17	Thornaby*	away		
,, 24	Northallerton*	away		
,, 31	Redcar*	home		
Sep. 7	North Ormesby	home		
,, 14	North Ormesby	away		
,, 21				
,, 28	Stockton	away		

* Denotes North Yorkshire League matches.

PATRONS:

Mrs. Chaloner	Rev. F. H. Morgan, M.A.
Miss Corney	Sir J. W. Pease, Bt., M.P.
J. W. Clarke, Esq., J.P.	A. E. Pease, Esq., J.P.
A. J. Dorman, Esq.	H. Fell Pease, Esq, M.P.
Rev. R. D. Eves, M.A.	Colonel Ropner
F. J. March, Esq.	W. C. Trevor, Esq.
J. Merryweather, Esq.	A. F. Watt, Esq.

OFFICIALS:

PRESIDENT—C. O. ORD, Esq.

VICE-PRESIDENTS—Major Richardson and Dr. S. H. Merryweather.

Captain 1st XI.—Mr. F. H. Merryweather.

Vice-Captain—Mr. J. Wicks.

Captain 2nd XI.—Mr. C. S. Musk.

Treasurer—Mr. T. Sanderson.

Auditor—Mr. G. W. Gaudie.

Joint Hon. Secs.—Messrs. H. Greear & G. H. Musk, 6, Chaloner Street, Guisbro'.

COMMITTEE:

G. W. Bulmer	W. Marshall
J. T. Brice	W. H. Sanderson
J. M. Grant	T. J. Woodcock
J. Kaye	R. Wright

Second Eleven Fixtures.

DATE.	NAME OF CLUB.	WHERE PLAYED	RESULT For	Agt
May 4	Redcar	home		
,, 11	Ironopolis	away		
,, 18	North Ormesby	home		
,, 25				
June 1				
,, 8	North Ormesby	away		
,, 15	Ironopolis	home		
,, 22				
,, 29	Thornaby	away		
July 6	Stockton Clarence	home		
,, 13				
,, 20	New Marske	away		
,, 27				
Aug. 3	Redcar	away		
,, 10	Stockton Clarence	away		
,, 17	Thornaby	home		
,, 24	New Marske	home		
,, 31	Marske	away		
Sep. 7				
,, 14	Marske	home		

Club Colours—MAROON AND GOLD.

Member's Subscription, 7/6.

Above: The membership card lists the officials at that time as: President, C. Ord; Vice-Presidents, Major Richardson and Dr S. Merryweather; Captain of the First XI, Mr F. Merryweather; Vice-Captain Mr J. Wicks; Captain of the Second X1, Mr C. Musk; Treasurer Mr T. Sanderson; Auditor Mr G. Gaudie.

Opposite, above: A party was held for the children of the Whitby Lane estate on the occasion of the Queen's Silver Jubilee, with games and sports and trestle tables heavily laden with food. Jonathon Edwards and Alec Smith, dressed as two of the Queen's Beefeaters, won a prize in the Fancy Dress competition.

Opposite below: Mr Robert Roland (Roley) Seaton proudly shows his prize-winning Bedlington Terrier. A magazine of the day states that, 'Mr R.R. Seaton's Bedlington Terrier Ch. Northcote Lucky Strike was the best in show at Cheltenham in 1961 and was the only bitch to have gained supreme honours during that year.'

The Anchor Inn on Belmangate, like most of the pubs in Guisborough, had its own cricket team and here are shown some of their members. Back row, from left to right: George Pallister, Brian Martin, -?- Brian Maughan, Les Hutchinson, George Willerton, Geoff Bailey. Front row: Don Appleton, Les Rooks, George Williams, Doug Haley, Bill Curry, John Barnard. On this day in 1970 they were celebrating winning the Saltburn British Legion Cup.

Opposite, above: Guisborough football team. Back row, from left to right: Harold Oliver, ? Smith, Noel Mason, -?- , -?- , -?- . Front row: -?- , -?- , Eric Trigg, -?- , -?- . The little mascot's name is unknown!

Opposite, below: The Quoit Club Eleven, winners in the mid-1960s of the Cricket Cup which was competed for by all the pubs and clubs in Guisborough. Back row, from left to right: Fred Dadd, Lennie McKnight, Alfie Edwards, Terry Mattews, Ernest Cottle. Middle row: Harold Oliver, Keith Robinson. Front row: Dougie Clements, Trevor Foster, 'Nobby' Boyes, Joe McGee, Colin Robinson.

The homecoming of Guisborough Town football team from Wembley, after playing there in April 1980.

The team gather in the garden of Sunnyfield House to greet their fans.

Above: What a welcome! It appears that the majority of Guisborough residents had gathered in Westgate to greet the footballers.

Right: A souvenir programme from 26 April 1980 when Guisborough Town played Stamford in the final of the FA Vase at Wembley. It was a great achievement and even though they lost the game they were given a heroes' welcome on their return home.

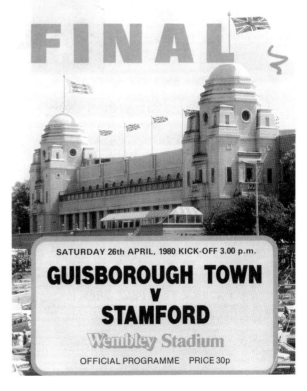

FOOTBALL ASSOCIATION CHALLENGE VASE

FINAL

SATURDAY 26th APRIL, 1980 KICK-OFF 3.00 p.m.

GUISBOROUGH TOWN
V
STAMFORD

Wembley Stadium

OFFICIAL PROGRAMME   PRICE 30p

Guisborough folk dancing team flushed with success after just winning the first prize at the competitions at Pocklington in 1946. From left to right: Mrs Dutton, Brenda Cleaver, Pat Abrahams, Peggy Bolton, Jean Young, -?- , Edna Wilson, Bertha Boyes, Clara Darnton, Avis Wesson (her father was the conductor of the

Priory band), Sheila Rowland and Beattie Hudson. The Guisborough folk dancers are still very active, meeting at Sunnyfield House on a regular basis.

After an exhausting walk from Guisborough, pulling a hand cart which contained everything needed to set up camp, these Scouts take a well-earned rest just below Highcliff.

Found amongst papers in the Grammar School archives, these two photographs have no names or date recorded, but judging by the style of clothes the author would take a guess at the 1950s.

seven

Schools

Senior boys of Northgate School proudly displaying the model of the market cross that they had just completed, *c.* 1935 Second from left at the back is Jack Wilson.

Guisborough Grammar School masters and pupils at the entrance to the school in 1900. The headmaster was Mr Eves, and the curate, on the right with a stick, was the Revd Mitchell.

Prize-giving and sports day at the Grammar School in 1934.

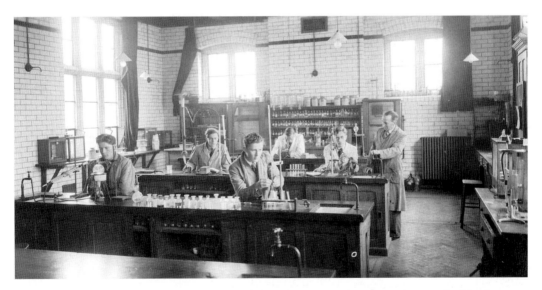

Inside the Chemistry laboratory at Guisborough Grammar School in 1952. This 1911 building became a student common room with the opening of the new Creative Arts/Science block in 1974. Back row, from left to right: Bob Robson, -?- , -?- , Mr Spedding. Front row: David Ferguson, Howard Smith.

Guisborough Grammar School cricket team. Back row from left to right: Barry Sanders, E. Harrison, Brian Westacott Second row: -?- , Geoff Farrington, -?- , Malcolm Gratton. Front row: Cliff Garbutt, Reg Darnton, Norman Robinson, -?- , -?-.

Northgate School, c. 1909. Somewhere on this picture is Walter Brelstaff, who will be remembered by many people in Guisborough, especially for his knowledge of local history. An excerpt from the school log book for that year states: 'Guisborough Infant School, May 18; The heating apparatus has been put on this morning. At 11.00 a.m. the water began to bubble out into the hand basins close to the cold water tank. The cloakroom filled with steam and as this continued I removed the children to the yard at 11.30. The cause of this was – no cold water in the tank, the tap being turned off.'

Northgate School 1932/3. Back row, from left to right: Victor Boyes, Frank Mitchell, ? Harland, Ronnie Boyes, Harry Eddon. Third row: ? Ord, Thora Hewling, Rene Gage, ? Weallans, Vera Brewer, ? Buckworth, -?- , ? Cole, Joan Sunley. Second row: Doreen Collier, Nan Robson, Sheila Rowlands, Doreen Trigg, Esther Armstrong. Front row: Margaret Newson, ? Sellars, Doris Hudson, Doreen Lines, Betty Swales, Joyce Edgecombe, ? Smith, Winnie Tucker, Joyce Carmen.

Pupils of Providence School in the 1930s perform the Operetta Fu Chang. The performance was held at the Temperance Hall.

Providence Infants' in 1948. Standing by the blackboard are Christine Young and Barbara Buxton, and seated left to right are: Maureen Milward, Janet Collins, David Willerton, -?- and Derek Richardson.

Northgate Junior School, 1951. Back row, from left to right: Bob Byers, John Watson, Keith Lorraine, Trevor Foster, Malcolm Charles, Jeff Hugill, Jeff Parker, Andy Sutcliffe, Eddy Winter, Alan Carter, Dave Willerton, Gordon Eaton, Derek Richardson. Third row: Myra Guite, Janet Collins, Anne Trenholme, Judith Bridges, Barbara Buxton, Paddy Booth, Cynthia Kidd, Eileen Curd, Christine Young, Barbara Compton, Joan Calvert, Olwyn Jones. Second row: Noreen Clements, Hilary Hodgeson, June Fawcett, Kathleen Swan, Barbara Wilkinson, Miss Mather, Judith ?, Ann Jackson, Nina Jackson, Elizabeth ?, Anne Johnstone. Front row: Alan Dale, Ronnie Allen, Derrick Richardson, Geoff Bowmaker, Jimmy Parkin, George Postgate. The school log book for 29 November 1951 records that 'A portion of the ceiling in Room 3 fell down this morning at approx. 9.50 a.m. and hit a teacher on the head. A doctor was sent for and he thought that as far as he could tell there was no serious damage'.

Providence School in 1952. Back row, from left to right: Derek Smith, Jeff Rutleigh, Freddie Suckling, William Topham, Ronnie Pearson, Barry Mitchell, Derek Fishpool, ? Tooley, Eric White. Third row: Brian Nixon, Billy Scase, Monica Blake, -?- , Jean Antil, -?- , -?- , Barbara Kerr, Derek Bulmer, Les Franks, Brian Tuttle. Second row: Ann Weldon, Doreen Humphries, -?- , -?- , -?- , Miss Coulthard, -?- , -?- , -?- , Pat Parker, Margaret Barnard. Front row: -?- , Kenny Watson, Tony Parkin.

Northgate School in the 1950s. Pupils include Kathleen Hall, Pat Townsend, Rob Bennett, Elsie Thompson, Tony Chocamenko, John Crowley, Jean England, Eric Buxton and Susan Guy.

Providence School in 1956. Back row, from left to right: ? Walker, Brian Judson, Graham Telford, Geoff Parker, Geoff Bowmaker, Herbert Carter, Ronnie Allen. Middle row: Dave Willerton, Bobby Byers, ? Hirst, June Fawcett, Trixie Chapman, -?- , Cynthia Kydd, Trevor Foster, Alan Dale, Terry Brown. Front row: Anne Johnson, Marian Wilkinson, Noreen Clements, -?- , Pat Brown, teacher Mr Basil Simpson, Pauline Leather, -?- , Dora Boone, Pauline Inman, ? Boyes.

THE PIRATES OF PENZANCE

OR

THE SLAVE OF DUTY

by

W. S. GILBERT AND ARTHUR SULLIVAN

(produced by permission of ~~R. D'Oyly Carte, Esq.~~)

Bridget D'Oyly Carte.

Dramatis Personae

Major-General Stanley	...	Mr. H. O. Arnott
The Pirate King	...	J. B. Snowdon
Samuel (his Lieutenant)	...	Mr. K. Spedding
Frederic (the Pirate Apprentice)	...	R. G. Ditchburn
Sergeant of Police	...	Mr. C. M. Sherrell
(General Mabel	...	D. S. Kehoe
Stanley's Edith	...	R. Padget
Daughters) Kate	...	M. Hore
Isabel	...	J. Nellist
Ruth (Pirate Maid of all work)	...	T. O. L. Weatleans

CHORUS OF PIRATES AND POLICE :

TENORS:—Mr. P. E. Moore, Mr. N. M. Noble, A. E. Bennett, B. F. Cleaver, D. J. Flower, T. M. Kehoe, T. Mackenzie, M. L. Midgley, A. Myers, J. A. Thrower, M. Whitlock.

BASSES:—Mr. W. P. Cooper, Mr. G. Farrington, Mr. I. Thomas, P. A. Boyt, G. Calitis, E. H. Laverick, A. Legg, D. Taylor, D. M. Wilson.

CHORUS OF GENERAL STANLEY'S DAUGHTERS:

D. G. Buttery, I. Mackenzie, B. Pette, J. R. Barker, M. Charles, E. Crossman, L. Hodgson, D. R. Lloyd, A. Smith, J. N. Barber, C. I. Beadon, K. R. Booth, M. Dadd, K. Fawcett, J. Hurst, G. S. Hinds, K. Hodgson, M. R. Kirby, B. Winspear.

Accompanist : Mrs. R. J. Routh

Scenery by: Miss E. M. Hood, A. Camidge, A. Myers

Lighting and Stage: Mr. E. Moreland, R. Blacklock, D. A. Rowe, D. W. Williams

ACT I—A ROCKY SEASHORE ON THE COAST OF CORNWALL

ACT II—A RUINED CHAPEL BY MOONLIGHT

God Save the Queen.

Left: A souvenir programme for the 1953 performance by Guisborough Grammar School boys of Gilbert and Sullivan's *Pirates of Penzance*. Several of these productions, including Iolanthe and The Mikado, were given by the pupils and staff of the boys' school, and the following pictures give credence to the fact that many grandfathers today were once 'fairies and bridesmaids'! (to quote David Flower)

Opposite, below: The cast of *Pirates of Penzance*, including from left to right: -?- , -?- , -?-, W.P. Cooper, C. Sherall, -?- , I. Thomas.

Actors, from left to right: Terry Weallans, Mr W.O. Arnott and J.B. Snowdon.

Pirates of Penzance, 1953.

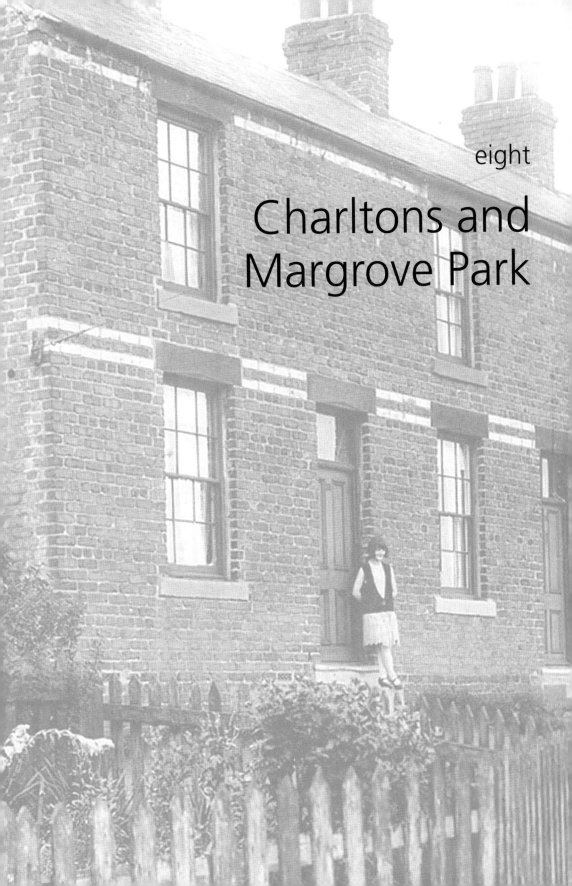

eight

Charltons and Margrove Park

In the foreground of this image is the Fox and Hounds Inn at Slapewath, with the railway line running past, and in the distance is Charltons and Margrove Park.

Charltons and the surrounding countryside, viewed from the top of Birk Brow.

Charltons before the demolition of the third row of houses.

A long row of terraced houses at Margrove Park, *c.* 1930.

Spawood Mine.

Sports day for the children of Charltons and Margrove Park in the 1930s.

Children from Charltons and 'Magra' at Margrove Park School with their football team in 1928. Back row, from left to right: Mr Hanley, Mr MacKenzie, -?- , -?- , Mrs Wilson, -?- , Miss Sprintall, -?- , Mr Sanderson, Mr Baker. The only children known are: front row on the left, Jack Balls; and extreme right Lil Cottle. Mr Wrightson, teacher, is seated at the right.

Pupils of Margrove Park School, 1929. Middle row, sixth from left is the only child identified, Lil Cottle. In the background is the wooden building which was Skidmore's fish and chip shop.

Members of Charltons brass band at Aysdale Gate. Always in great demand the band would, on occasion, have two engagements for the same day, but that was no problem as they simply divided themselves up, each half playing at different venues. They were disbanded before the war, which makes this photograph pre-1939. On the extreme right is Robert Alderson.

The billiards players stand outside the Mission at Charltons, c. 1912. Back row, from left to right: John Day, Arthur (Sandy) Balls, Burt Nixon, Ernie Balls. Middle row (standing): Alf Barnes, Nat Smith. Front row: Arthur Friston and Bob Brookes.

Charlton's Mission footballers in the early twentieth century.

Margrove Park School, *c.* 1957. Back row, from left to right: John Pearey, John Blows, Michael Wynn, Peter Jacques, John Young, Geoffrey Wetherell, Geoffrey Ovington, John Bennison, George McGee, Eric Dadd, Barry Dixon, Alan Leng. Middle row: Jeannie Hancock, Heather Young, Margaret Rix, Alan Calvert, Marion Miller, Charles Alderson, Joan Hardman, Kit Armstrong, Joan Calvert, June Pattison. Front row: Carol Pickering, Cheryl Rye, Joan Leng, Barbara Bright, Pat Smith, Mr Clayman, Pat Noddings, Freda Leng, Edna Miller, Rita Pickering, Valerie Ovington.

Margrove Park School football team. Back row, from left to right: Barry Dixon, George McGee, Charles Alderson, John Tucker, Geoff Wetherell, John Young. Front row: John Blows, Alan Jones, Alan Calvert, Peter Jacques, Michael Wynn.

When is a wedding not a wedding? When it's a day out to Gretna Green! Friends and neighbours from Charltons and Margrove Park on a day trip to Scotland stage a mock shotgun wedding which was enjoyed by all. Several people have been named, but with such a crowded picture perhaps the best thing is to make a list: 'Bride' and 'Groom' are Lilian Taylor and Jack Dixon; 'Father' with the shotgun is Mr Milner; seated on the left is Percy Wilson and beside him, kneeling, is the coach driver Mr Wakefield. Others include Mr and Mrs Wakefield Snr, Muriel Jacques, Dorothy Prout, Peggy Wetherell, Ann Lobley, Barbara Hancock, Katy Wetherell, Kit Armstrong and Lil Wilson (née Cottle).

In 1984 Kevin Keegan came to Boosbeck to open the new community centre.

Spawood cottages in the early twentieth century. To the left of the houses are the railway wagons that carried iron ore down from the mines. Spawood mines extended over a large area, running beneath the hills as far as Commondale.

'Ye old Spa', the health spa where people came to take the waters, and which gave rise to the name Spawood.

The newly-built powder house at Spawood Mine, *c.* 1900.

Ironstone miners, *c.* 1890.

Miners at the top of Spawood shale heap, at the turn of the twentieth century.

Very young miners at Spawood Belt, *c.* 1913.

This was one of, if not the last day of Chaloner Pit in 1938. It must have been a time of mixed feelings – sadness at seeing the end of an era and at the loss of jobs – and yet relief at no longer having to go deep underground to do such dangerous work.

Miners at the entrance to Spawood Drift Mine, possibly about to begin a shift as their hands and faces are clean, quite the opposite of when the shift was ending and they headed home.

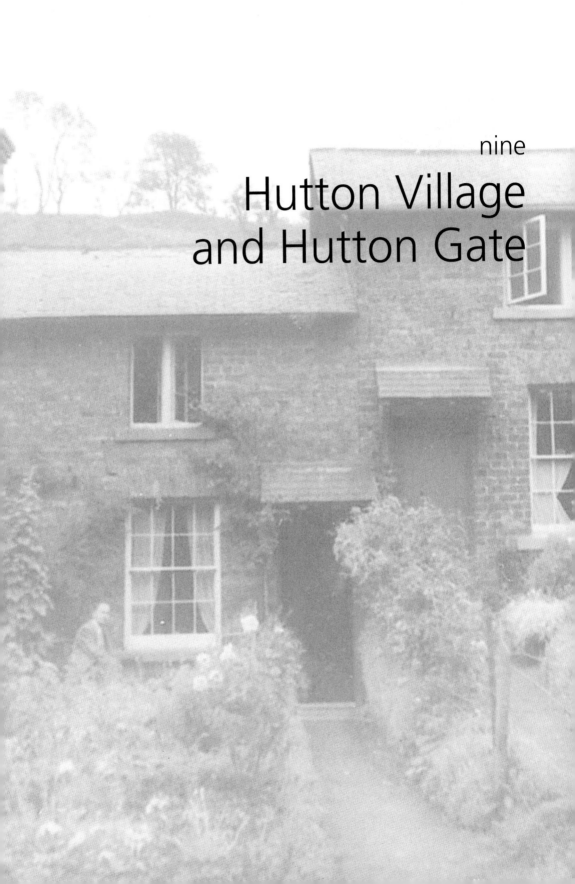

nine

Hutton Village
and Hutton Gate

Hutton Lowcross village as seen from the Kildale Track, *c.* 1955.

Above: Children of Hutton school in a Christmas concert, c. 1953. Back row, from left to right: Pat Brown, Carole Devon, Pauline Inman, –?– , Dorothy Boston, –?– , Jennifer Fulton, Lorraine East, Jennifer Deadman, Irene Ward. Front row: Brenda Jackson, Hilary Jeffels, Pamela Marshall, possibly Nigel Cornier as Santa Claus, John Topham, Christine Naseby, Pat Williams.

Left: The cottages of Hutton village in 1954 had barely altered from the day when they were built, although by this time they did have the addition of electricity, which had been introduced in around 1950.